NERDY BABIES

SPACE

EMMY KASTNER

ROARING BROOK PRESS

NEW YORK

Hello, Nerdy Babies!
Do you ever wonder about

SPACE ?

You probably do.
You're curious.

Look up!

Way, way, _way_ up . . .

Above your roof,

beyond the trees,

past the clouds . . .

you'll find outer space.

STARS

DARK
AND
COLD

There's no gravity here!
Gravity keeps everything
on the ground back on Earth.

There's no sound in space.

Planets spin,
stars sparkle,
and comets
silently fly by.

This is our sun.
It's the center of
our solar system,
and it's very bright.

HOT!

In the time it takes to get from one birthday to the next, Earth makes one lap around the sun.

Do you love the moon?
Earth sure does!

They travel around
space together.

There's no wind on the moon.
Your footprints will last forever.

There are eight planets
in our solar system.

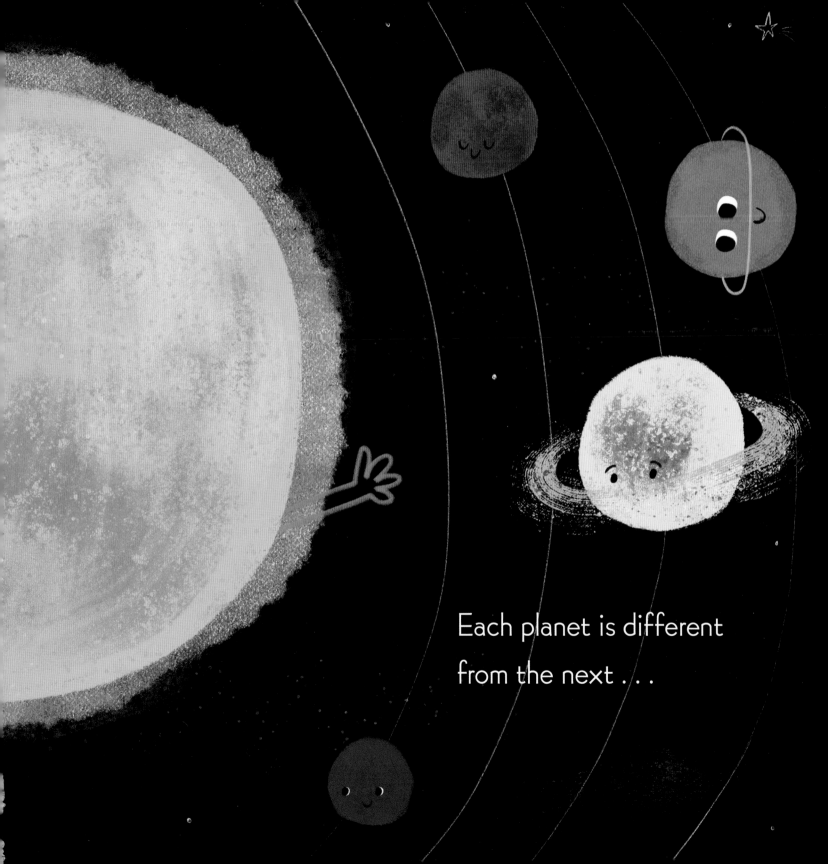

Each planet is different

from the next . . .

MERCURY is the smallest planet and closest to the sun.

SUN

VENUS

spins backward!

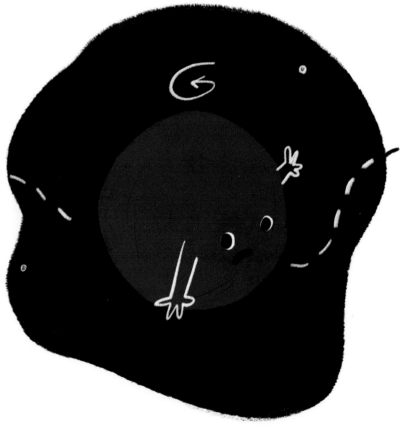

EARTH!

The only planet that supports life in our solar system . . . yet!

The tallest mountain in
the solar system is on **MARS!**

JUPITER has 79 moons!

Pluto used to be
called a planet.

WE STILL
LOVE you!

SATELLITES
LIKE THIS
ORBIT PLANETS
AND COLLECT
DATA.

We learn more about
our solar system and the
whole universe every day!

Astronauts look up to the sky and ask a lot of questions—

just like you!

NERDY
ASTRONAUT
↓

NERDY
KID
↓

NERDY
BABY
↓

EARTH

STAY CURIOUS!

There's more to learn
about everything.

For Dan—forever supportive, and future Mars pioneer

Copyright © 2019 by Emmy Kastner
Published by Roaring Brook Press
Roaring Brook Press is a division of Holtzbrinck Publishing Holdings Limited Partnership
175 Fifth Avenue, New York, NY 10010
mackids.com

Library of Congress Control Number: 2018955663
ISBN: 978-1-250-31204-4

Our books may be purchased in bulk for promotional, educational, or business use. Please contact your local bookseller or the Macmillan Corporate and Premium Sales Department at (800) 221-7945 ext. 5442 or by email at MacmillanSpecialMarkets@macmillan.com.

First edition, 2019
Book design by Aram Kim
Printed in China by RR Donnelley Asia Printing Solutions Ltd., Dongguan City, Guangdong Province
1 3 5 7 9 10 8 6 4 2